MOST PEOPLE do not know that already enacted in current law for 2013 are increases in the top rates of virtually every major federal tax. That is because the tax increases of ObamaCare become effective that year, and the Bush tax cuts expire, which Obama has refused to renew for the nation's small businesses, job creators, and investors.

As a result, if the Bush tax cuts expire just for singles making over $200,000 per year and for couples making over $250,000, in 2013 the top two income tax rates will jump nearly 20 percent, the capital-gains tax rate will soar by nearly 60 percent, the tax on corporate dividends will nearly triple, and the Medicare payroll tax will leap by 62 percent for those disfavored taxpayers.

This is on top of the U.S. corporate income tax rate, which is virtually the highest in the industrialized world. The federal rate is 35 percent, with state corporate rates taking it close to 40 percent on average. But even Communist China has a 25 percent rate. The average rate in the heavily socialist European

Union is less than that. Formerly socialist Canada has a 16.5 percent rate, which will go down to 15 percent in 2012.

U.S. corporate tax rates leave American companies uncompetitive in the global economy. Yet under President Obama, there is no relief in sight. Instead, he continually proposes still further tax increases on American business.

Higher tax rates mean producers can only keep a smaller percentage of what they produce. So tax-rate increases reduce the incentive for productive activities – such as saving, investment, starting businesses, expanding businesses, job creation, entrepreneurship, and work – resulting in less of each. And that is what Barack Obama's tax tsunami for 2013 is going to do, which will swamp the weak economy.

Most small-business profits are reported from households earning more than $200,000/$250,000 per year, and those small businesses produce more than half the new jobs. So Obama's 2013 tax tsunami effectively targets

U.S. corporate tax rates leave American companies uncompetitive in the global economy.

small businesses and the nation's job creators. That will hurt working people the most because they will lose the jobs and the wage income they need to maintain their basic standard of living.

It is incentives to produce that drive the economy, which was the insight of Reagan - omics. Expand the incentives, and the economy will recover and boom. Weaken those incentives, and the economy will fall into further decline.

Obamanomics is based instead on the old-fashioned Keynesian economics of the 1930s to the 1970s, which holds that government spending and deficits are the foundation for economic recovery and prosperity. If that were true, then America would be enjoying its strongest economy ever right now. Government spending and deficits do not lead to economic growth and prosperity. Just the opposite.

Obama's Regulatory Blizzard

Besides imposing all these tax-rate increases and uncompetitive rates on American businesses large and small, the blizzard of new regulatory costs and barriers imposed by the Obama administration will be building to a crescendo by 2013 as well. Academic studies estimate the total costs of regulation in the economy to be rapidly rising toward $2 trillion per year, or $8,000 per employee. That is close to 10 times the corporate income tax burden and double the individual income tax. When the resulting effects on the economy are considered, the total losses due to regulatory burdens may total $3 trillion, or one-fifth of our entire economy.

But by 2013, these regulatory costs will have exploded in unprecedented fashion because of the regulatory blizzard coming from the Obama administration. Already, Obama and his minions have loaded up another 4,225 new federal regulations in the pipeline toward implementation. But the heavy regulatory artillery is just being wheeled into place.

The Environmental Protection Agency (EPA) is effectively imposing cap and trade by administrative regulation under the Clean Air Act – without congressional approval. They have already issued an "endangerment finding" that greenhouse gases threaten the public through global warming. But the Clean Air Act leaves little room for flexibility. That endangerment finding sets us on the road to ultimately banning any major carbon emissions from the burning of oil, natural gas, and coal. That would effectively repeal the Industrial Revolution: an environmental-extremist dream but a nightmare for working people and the economy. It would mean the end of the American Dream and of America's heritage of world-leading economic prosperity.

Though modern nuclear power plants are safe, the nuclear accident in Japan precludes increased reliance on nuclear power for the foreseeable future. And powering a modern, 21st century industrial economy with alternative energy from wind, solar, and biofuel is a fantasy rather than a dream. The energy content in these alternatives is highly diffuse, which means they are inherently costly and inefficient. That should not be surprising, because they are basically the power sources of the preindustrial Roman Empire 2,000 years ago.

They each require vast land areas for windmills, solar panels, or crops. They also require traditional power sources as a backup for when the wind doesn't blow or the sun doesn't shine, which would further add to the overwhelming costs. But if the endangerment finding means the phaseout of coal, natural gas, and oil, then there are not going to be any backup power sources.

The EPA is starting implementation of this

new, unprecedented regulatory burden by first targeting carbon emissions from major industrial plants and utilities, so the general public won't see the burden before the 2012 election. But this is going to start raising energy costs, making American manufacturing more uncompetitive in the global economy. In 2013 and thereafter, unless we change

---

Obamanomics is based on old-fashioned Keynesian economics, which holds that government spending and deficits are the foundation for economic recovery and prosperity.

---

course, the regulation will be expanded to affect virtually every business in the economy, large and small, every commercial facility, every significant building and office, every hospital and medical facility, every restaurant, even smaller fast-food operations. That will mean at a minimum trillions in new costs to the economy. A modern industrial economy cannot function over the long run under these requirements.

The EPA's "endangerment finding" providing the foundation for this regulation is subject to stiff legal challenges winding their way through the courts, which contend that the finding is not sufficiently supported by proven science. And well it should be challenged. The most authoritative critique of the theory that human activity is causing potentially catastrophic global warming is the 856-page *Climate Change Reconsidered*, published by the Heartland Institute in 2009. This careful, thoroughly scientific volume co-authored by dozens of fully credentialed scientists comprehensively addresses every aspect of global warming, showing that natural causes are primarily responsible for climate patterns of the past century. Heartland has just published a follow-up interim report addressing new developments.

These publications alone establish at a minimum that the theory that human activity is causing potentially catastrophic global warming is in fact hotly disputed among knowledgeable scientists. But recent findings effectively prove that the notion of man-caused global warming is false. Published peer-reviewed papers by Richard Lindzen, Alfred P. Sloan Professor of Meteorology at the Massachusetts Institute of Technology, find that a doubling of carbon dioxide (CO_2) in the atmosphere (currently up only 44 percent from preindustrial levels) would increase temperatures by 0.7 degrees Kelvin, less than half the estimate of the theoretical climate models used by the U.N.'s Intergovernmental Panel on Climate Change (IPCC), on which the EPA exclusively relies.

Another published paper by Roy Spencer, U.S. science team leader for the AMSR-E instrument flying on NASA's Aqua satellite and the principal research scientist for the

Earth System Science Center at the University of Alabama at Huntsville, uses atmospheric temperature data from NASA's Terra satellite to show that much more heat escapes back out to space than is assumed to be captured in the atmosphere by greenhouse effects under the U.N.'s theoretical climate models. This explains why the warming temperature changes predicted by the U.N.'s global-warming models over the past 20 years have been so much greater than the actual measured temperature changes.

In August 2011 came the results of a major experiment by the European Organization for Nuclear Research (CERN) involving 63 scientists from 17 European and U.S. institutes. The results show that the sun's cosmic rays resulting from sunspots have a much greater effect on Earth's temperatures through their effect on cloud cover than the U.N.'s global warming models have been assuming. This helps to explain why the historical pattern of temperature changes seems to follow the rise and fall of sunspots rather than the concentration of CO_2 in the atmosphere. This further confirms what Heartland's *Climate Change Reconsidered* argues – that natural causes, not greenhouse gases, have the dominant effect on Earth's temperatures.

Finally, the U.N.'s own climate models project that if man's greenhouse-gas emissions were causing global warming, there would be a particular pattern of temperature distribution in the atmosphere, which scientists call the fingerprint. Temperatures in the troposphere portion of the atmosphere above the tropics would increase with altitude, producing a "hotspot" near the top of the troposphere, about 6 miles above the earth's surface. Above that, in the stratosphere, there would be cooling. But higher-quality temperature data from weather balloons and satellites now show just the opposite: no increasing warming with altitude in the troposphere above the tropics but rather a slight cooling, with no hotspot, no fingerprint.

So the scientific foundation for the EPA's shutting down our modern, 21st century industrial economy has been obliterated. But that is not stopping them, because of the extremist ideology and special interests driving the global-warming charade.

This is just the beginning of the sweeping regulatory costs the Obama administration is imposing. The EPA has formally proposed for implementation a maximum achievable control technology regulation that would require utilities to reduce mercury emissions from U.S. power plants from 29 tons a year to 5. Yet the EPA's own scientific studies conclude that reducing mercury emissions from all sources by as much as 41 tons would be unlikely to substantially affect health risks.

Coal-fired power plants produce about 50 percent of the nation's electricity. The Edison Electric Institute estimates that the regulatory costs imposed by Obama's EPA would force more than one-fourth of these power plants to close, with $200 billion in additional costs for those remaining open. As William Yeatman writes in the *New York Post* on Aug. 9, 2011, "The loss of that much power production makes brownouts and rolling blackouts a virtual certainty in some regions of the country," with the added costs resulting in "higher US electricity prices – which will push up the costs of every business in America." Unions filing comments on the EPA's proposed regulations estimate a direct loss of a quarter of a million jobs. EPA's just-issued cross-state emissions restrictions will result in shutting down additional power plants. America is powering down.

The EPA has also proposed a final regulation that would ban the coal-mining technique of mountaintop removal, claiming that resulting salt runoff harms a short-lived insect. Yeatman explains that this would "outlaw an industry that employs more than 15,000 miners in Appalachia." He adds, "These are just a few examples of a host of unjustified EPA measures targeted at coal. The obvious goal is to seize any excuse to make coal power more expensive – eventually, as then-candidate Barack Obama put it to the San Francisco Chronicle in 2008, to

The scientific foundation for the EPA's shutting down our modern, 21st century industrial economy has been obliterated.

'bankrupt' the coal industry." That would result in higher electricity costs for businesses, particularly energy-intensive manufacturing, across the board.

The Obama administration is restricting oil production as well. The unnecessary and legally unjustifiable Gulf oil-drilling moratorium imposed in response to the Deepwater Horizon oil leak in 2010 still has not been lifted, causing oil-drilling rigs to leave American waters for opportunities off the coasts of other countries. When Exxon announced it had discovered a new oil field in the Gulf holding an estimated 1 billion barrels of oil, which would be the largest Gulf oil field ever, the Obama administration responded that Exxon's leases for the fields had expired, and it denied an extension that had traditionally been routine. Obama shut down already approved and permitted drilling off the coast of Alaska as well. Even oil-shale production on land in the American West has been restricted.

Pending before the Obama administration for its entire three years has been approval for the proposed Keystone XL pipeline, which would bring Canadian crude oil to Texas refineries on the Gulf Coast. That would involve more than a million barrels a day, more than is imported from Saudi Arabia or Venezuela, ultimately producing a quarter of a million new jobs in the energy industry alone. But Obama's green base opposes it vociferously. Now projects are under way to transport Canadian oil to the Pacific to supply Asia, including our booming rival China.

These restricted energy supplies are killing jobs directly in the American energy industry, losses that will only mount over time.

More broadly, the result will be lower energy supplies at higher costs than otherwise for the American economy, killing many more jobs.

Moreover, in 2010 Obama led the passage of the Dodd-Frank financial regulatory reform legislation. That provides authorization for hundreds of new costly regulations on the financial community over the next year that will further squelch the credit for businesses and consumers essential to restoring economic growth and recovery. As Rep. Scott Garrett (R-N.J.) wrote in *Investor's Business Daily* on July 21:

> *Since the passage of Dodd-Frank, credit conditions continue to be tight . . . and massive regulatory overreach is making the cost of doing business at every level in the supply chain more expensive for main street businesses. . . . Even more alarming, a number of these businesses have said that if certain proposed regulations become final in their current form, then they will be forced to leave the markets altogether to avoid the regulatory costs imposed by Dodd-Frank. . . . [W]e have severely impaired the global competi-*

tiveness of the U.S. financial markets and pushed companies to take their capital and jobs to friendlier terrain overseas.

In June, JPMorgan CEO Jamie Dimon asked Fed Chairman Ben Bernanke if anyone was keeping track of the costs of all of the Obama administration's new and proposed regulations on the financial community. As *The Wall Street Journal* commented on June 16, 2011, "Mr. Bernanke admitted that the regulators don't have a clue. 'It's just too complicated,' he said, in a remark for the history books."

Investor's Business Daily added on Aug. 16, "Shortly after Dodd-Frank's 2,500 pages became law, the American Bankers Association warned that its 'tsunami of regulations' would wipe out hundreds of smaller banks." Small banks cannot absorb the costs of complex new regulations like big banks can. If your bank has only 19 employees, they don't have time to even read voluminous new federal regulations, let alone implement them. As a result, some small banks are already starting to shut down because of the costly new requirements of

Dodd-Frank. That growing trend will further deny small businesses, new start-ups, and local communities access to essential credit. But even big banks are already laying off workers under the new regulatory cost burdens.

President Obama touted Dodd-Frank to America as permanently ending any further taxpayer bailouts for too-big-to-fail financial firms. But the truth is, instead of ending all such bailouts, Dodd-Frank institutionalized them with permanent federal authority for still further bailouts. The act gives the FDIC authority to lend to a failing financial firm, purchase the assets of a failing financial firm, guarantee the obligations of a failing financial firm, and pay off its creditors.

The FDIC can finance this with permanent authority to borrow up to 90 percent of the fair value of the failed firm's total consolidated assets from the U.S. Treasury, meaning you, the taxpayers. For Bank of America, for JPMorgan Chase, for Citigroup, that could amount to $2 trillion *each*.

The markets are telling us that they recognize this as permanent bailout authority, charging banks identified as too big to fail 78 basis points less for their borrowed funds than others. So while Dodd-Frank imposes costs that will harm smaller banks relatively more than bigger banks, it also grants big banks a permanent competitive advantage with government-backed lower-cost funds. President Obama's rhetoric on Dodd-Frank has been abusively dishonest.

Then there are all the regulatory costs of ObamaCare's coming on line. Vast new realms of regulation are already starting to increase the cost of health insurance for employers and others, and that is only just beginning. The employer mandate yet to become effective will require employers to buy the most expensive health insurance possible for their workers, with all of the politically correct regulatory requirements imposed on it. That is already causing employers to delay hiring, and once it all becomes effective, layoffs will soar further. Smaller businesses will cut back to fall below the 50-worker threshold at which the employer mandate applies, and companies below that threshold will hold back their growth. The rising cost of health insurance across the board will be a new drain on the economy.

But these are just the highlights of the building reregulation blizzard from the Obama administration that will sharply increase costs and slash business creation, expansion, and the resulting jobs in manufacturing, mining, oil and gas production and refining, chemical plants, communications, utilities, railroads, airlines, diesel transportation, coal production and use, lithium-battery production, and agriculture. Additional problems and costs arise out of antitrust and OSHA reregulation.

The Fed and the Coming Recession

Then there is the Fed and the effects of its monetary policy. The Obama administration has cheered on the Fed's loose-as-a-bordello monetary policy, with near-zero interest rates for years now and the printing presses cranking out reams of cheap money. That loose policy cannot simply be ended after years without an economic downturn. Investors are misled by the money expansion and artificially low interest rates to make investments that are dependent on those policies. When those policies end, so does the economic foundation of their investments. The result is higher unemployment – and a recession. That was the pattern of the 1970s, which was the last time we followed the same Keynesian economic policies of the Obama administration.

That is why the Fed has announced that it will continue its near-zero interest policies until 2013. The Fed doesn't need to call it QE3 to run a monetary policy of economic crack that will hold the economy on a false high from what it would be through the election, which is what Texas Governor Rick Perry – as well as former House Speaker Newt Gingrich – has correctly criticized.

But the loose monetary policy has to end at some point, or the result will be ruinous inflation. The CPI already soared in July 2011 at an 8 percent annual rate. And the 1970s proved that we can have double-digit inflation and recession at the same time.

To keep inflation from getting out of control, the Fed will end its wildly loose monetary policy after the 2012 elections. The contractionary effect of that will hit in 2013 at the same time as all the tax-rate increases, and all the exploding regulatory costs, discussed above.

Art Laffer predicted the coming crash of 2011 on the basis of the expiration of the Bush tax cuts on the upper-income earners alone. Those tax-rate increases were extended to 2013 in December 2010 out of fear that the prediction was right. But now in 2013, in addition to those tax-rate increases, we have all of the tax increases of ObamaCare, the further exploding costs of Obama's building regulatory blizzard, and the contractionary effect of the Fed's monetary policies. Unless we reverse course, the result will be one big, bad crash in 2013.

* * *

But none of this has to be. America is not in some permanent decline. It is being trashed by bad policies. If those policies are reversed and replaced by progrowth, free-market principles, the American economy can be booming again within a year.

In fact, economic recovery is long overdue. Before this last recession and since the Great Depression, recessions in America have lasted an average of 10 months, with the longest previously lasting 16 months.

But in August 2011, *44 months* after the last recession began, unemployment was stuck at 9.1 percent, with exactly zero jobs created for the month, leaving more than 25 million Americans unemployed or underemployed. This is the longest period of unemployment that high since the Great Depression, when Keynesian economics first reigned supreme.

Unemployment for African Americans was 16.7 percent, stuck at depression levels for more than two years. Hispanic unemployment, at 11.3 percent, has been in double digits for more than two years as well. Teenage unemployment was at a depression-level 25.4 percent. Black teenage unemployment was at a Jim Crow-level 46.5 percent.

The U6 unemployment rate, reflecting total unemployment and underemployment, was 16.2 percent. And that still doesn't fully count the millions of Americans who have given up and dropped out of the workforce altogether.

Then on Sept. 13 came the Census Bureau report fleshing out the full meaning of no economic recovery under Obama. Median family income has fallen all the way back to 1996 levels. *The Wall Street Journal* further reported on Sept. 14, "Earnings of the typical man who works full-time year round fell, and are lower – adjusted for inflation – than in 1978."

The poverty rate climbed to 15.1 percent, higher than in the late 1960s when the War on Poverty was getting under way, $16 trillion ago. The child poverty rate climbed to 22 percent – nearly a quarter of all American children. The total number of Americans in poverty is higher than at any time in the more than 50 years that the Census Bureau has been tallying poverty. Moreover, the number of Americans ages 25-34 living with their parents has soared by 25 percent.

Obama apologists cannot argue that this is because the recession he inherited was so bad. The historical record for the American economy is that the worse the downturn, the stronger the recovery. Based on the historical record, we should be completing our second year of a booming recovery by now.

Reaganomics vs. Obamanomics

As I explain in my recent book, *America's Ticking Bankruptcy Bomb*, in order to see how we can achieve another economic boom, we need to look at what we did the last time America got into such trouble. When President Reagan entered office in 1981, he actually faced much worse economic problems than President Obama faced in 2009. Three worsening recessions starting in 1969 were about to culminate in the worst of all in 1981-82, with unemployment soaring into double digits at a peak of 10.8 percent. At the same time, America suffered roaring double-digit inflation, with inflation raging at 11.3 percent in 1979 and 13.5 percent in 1980 (25 percent in two years). The Washington establishment at the time argued that this inflation had become endemic to the American economy and could not be stopped, at least not without a calamitous economic collapse.

The Obama administration has cheered on the Fed's loose-as-a-bordello monetary policy.

This was accompanied by double-digit interest rates, with the prime rate peaking at 21.5 percent in 1980. The poverty rate started increasing in 1978, eventually climbing by a third from 11.4 percent to 15.2 percent. A fall in real median family income that began in 1978 snowballed to a decline of almost 10 percent by 1982. In addition, from 1968 to 1982, the Dow lost 70 percent of its real value, reflecting an overall collapse of stocks.

President Reagan campaigned on an explicitly articulated, four-point economic program to reverse this slow-motion collapse of the American economy:

1. **Tax *rates* cut** to restore incentives for economic growth. That was implemented first with a reduction in the top income tax rate of 70 percent down to 50 percent, and then a 25 percent across-the-board reduction in income tax rates for everyone. The 1986 tax reform then reduced tax rates further, leaving just two rates, 28 percent and 15 percent.

2. **Spending reductions**, implemented first by a $31 billion cut in spending in 1981, close to 5 percent of the federal budget then, or the equivalent of about $185 billion

in spending cuts for the year today. In constant dollars, nondefense discretionary spending declined by 14.4 percent from 1981 to 1982 and by 16.8 percent from 1981 to 1983. Moreover, in constant dollars, this nondefense discretionary spending never returned to its 1981 level for the rest of Reagan's two terms. Even with the Reagan defense buildup, which won the Cold War without firing a shot, total federal spending declined from a high of 23.5 percent of GDP in 1983 to 21.3 percent in 1988 and 21.2 percent in 1989. That's a real reduction in the size of government, relative to the economy, of 10 percent.

3. **Deregulation**, which saved consumers an estimated $100 billion per year in lower prices. Reagan's first executive order, in fact, eliminated price controls on oil and natural gas. Production soared, and the price of oil declined by more than 50 percent.

4. **Anti-inflation monetary policy** restraining money supply growth compared with

demand, to maintain a stable value of the dollar.

These economic policies amounted to the most successful experiment in world history. The Reagan recovery started in official records in November 1982 and lasted 92 months without a recession until July 1990, when the tax increases of the 1990 budget deal killed it. That set a new record for the longest peacetime expansion ever, the previous high being 58 months.

During this seven-year recovery, the economy grew by almost one-third, the equivalent of adding the entire economy of West Germany, the third-largest in the world at the time, to the U.S. economy. In 1984 alone, real economic growth boomed by 6.8 percent, the highest in 50 years. Nearly 20 million new jobs were created during those seven years of recovery, increasing U.S. civilian employment by almost 20 percent, with unemployment falling to 5.3 percent by 1989. In contrast, today we are still 7 million jobs below the peak before the last recession started almost four years ago.

The shocking rise in inflation during the Carter years was extinguished at the same time, contrary to the establishment economists initially laughing at Reaganomics. Inflation in 1980 was reduced by more than half, to 6.2 percent, by 1982 and cut in half again, to 3.2 percent, by 1983, never to be heard from again until recently. The contractionary, tight-money policies needed to kill this inflation inexorably created the steep recession of 1981 to 1982, which is why Reagan did not suffer politically catastrophic blame for that recession.

Real per capita disposable income increased by 18 percent from 1982 to 1989, meaning America's standard of living increased by almost 20 percent in just seven years. The poverty rate declined every year from 1984 to 1989, dropping by one-sixth from its peak. The stock market more than tripled in value from 1980 to 1990, a larger increase than in any previous decade.

In *The End of Prosperity*, supply-side guru Laffer and *Wall Street Journal* chief financial writer Stephen Moore point out that this Reagan recovery grew into a 25-year boom, with just slight interruptions of shallow, short recessions in 1990 and 2001. They wrote:

> *We call this period, 1982–2007, the twenty-five year boom – the greatest period of wealth creation in the history of the planet. In 1980, the net worth – assets minus liabilities – of all U.S. households and business . . . was $25 trillion in today's dollars. By 2007 . . . net worth was just shy of $57 trillion. Adjusting for inflation, more wealth was created in America in the twenty-five year boom than in the previous two hundred years.*

What is so striking about Obamanomics is how it so doggedly pursues the opposite of every one of the planks of Reaganomics. Instead of reducing tax rates, President Obama is committed to raising the top tax rates of virtually every major federal tax in 2013, as discussed above. The only major tax rate not already to be increased under current law is the federal corporate tax rate of 35 percent, which is already way too high, as also discussed above.

Instead of coming into office with spending cuts, President Obama's first act was the massive, nearly $1 trillion stimulus bill. In his first three years in office, he has already increased federal spending by 28 percent, and his 2012 budget proposed to increase federal spending by another 57 percent by 2021. Now he has proposed further spending increases, calling it a jobs plan.

Instead of deregulation, we have across-the-board reregulation, from health care to finance to energy and elsewhere. While Reagan used to say that his energy policy was to "unleash the private sector," Obama's energy policy can be described as precisely to leash the private sector in service to Obama's central-planning "green energy" dictates.

Obama's monetary policy is just the opposite of Reagan's as well. Instead of restraining the money supply to match money demand for a stable dollar, slaying a historic inflation, we have QE1 and QE2 and a steadily collapsing dollar, arguably creating a historic reflation.

This is why there has been no recovery. And pursuing the opposite of Reaganomics in great detail is why we are on track for the opposite results of Reaganomics, with the coming crash of 2013.

Restoring the American Dream

To restore booming economic recovery and growth, we only need to restore each of the four planks of Reaganomics, updated for today.

Tax Rates. For tax rates, that means tax reform for individual and family taxpayers and, for corporate taxpayers, closing loopholes in return for lowering rates. House Budget Committee Chairman Paul Ryan proposed in his 2012 budget, which has already passed the House, tax reform for individuals and families providing for a top income tax rate of 25 percent for families making over

$100,000 a year, and a 10 percent tax rate for families making less. A generous standard deduction of $25,000 for couples and $12,500 for singles, and a personal exemption of $3,500 per family member, would exempt the first $39,000 per year for a family of four from any income tax.

Ryan's budget also included corporate tax reform that would reduce the federal corporate tax rate from 35 percent to 25 percent. In return, the proposed reforms would close the many corporate tax loopholes that allowed Obama corporate crony General Electric to escape paying any taxes on $14 billion in corporate profits.

In my book *America's Ticking Bankruptcy Bomb*, I proposed a 15 percent flat tax for indi-

---

America is not in some permanent decline. It is being trashed by bad policies.

---

vidual and family taxpayers and a 15 percent federal tax rate for corporations. Between the revenues saved by closing loopholes and the new revenues generated by the booming economic growth resulting from the lower rates, such reform could quite possibly end up generating more revenues than the current tax system.

But any resulting shortfall could be made up by spending reductions. The top priority is to adopt tax reforms that would maximize economic growth and jobs and get the American economy booming again with world-leading prosperity. Federal spending then must be shoehorned into the revenues that tax code produces.

The American income tax code suffers from the multiple taxation of capital, which means that capital income is taxed several times. It is taxed once by the corporate income tax when it is earned. Whatever is paid in dividends is taxed a second time by the individual income tax. When the value of the capital interest increases – a share of stock, for example – it is taxed again by the capital-gains tax. If anything is left at death, it is subject to taxation again by the death tax.

This multiple taxation of capital discourages investment, which is what creates jobs and bids up wages by making workers more productive. With a corporate income tax, capital income should not be taxed a second and third time as capital gains and dividends. That means ideally that the capital-gains tax should be zero, as it is for many of our international competitors, and dividends should be tax exempt as well. But even keeping the Bush tax rates of 15 percent for capital gains and dividends would be workable.

The death tax, however, should be abolished as an unfair additional layer of taxation on a lifetime of savings that has already been taxed a number of times. The same is true for the alternative minimum tax (AMT), which was adopted in the late 1960s to ensure that top-income taxpayers pay some tax. But now it is applying to more moderate-income taxpayers, and with the above tax reforms closing unfair loopholes, there would no longer be any role for the AMT.

Spending. The first step in getting spending under control is to implement the Ryan budget that was already approved by the House. That budget would reduce domestic federal spending to below 2008 levels and cut $6.2 trillion in spending in the first 10 years alone.

It would defund and repeal ObamaCare, eliminate hundreds of duplicative programs, and slash corporate welfare. That would include President Obama's "expensive handouts for uncompetitive sources of energy," establishing instead "a free and open marketplace for energy development, innovation and exploration," as Ryan explained in the April 5, 2011, *Wall Street Journal.* Ryan also explained that his budget "gets rid of the permanent Wall Street bailout authority that Congress created last year" in President Obama's Dodd-Frank so-called financial regulatory reform bill.

Federal spending would be reduced to below 20 percent of GDP, the long-run postwar historical average over the past 60 years, by 2015. Yet Ryan's tax reforms would restore federal revenues to their long-run postwar historical average of about 18 percent of GDP. That means the budget would be permanently balanced after a dozen years or so, continuing eventually to pay off the national debt entirely, as scored by the Congressional Budget Office.

Those results can be accelerated by further abolishing and consolidating federal departments and agencies. The Departments of Agriculture, HUD, Labor, and Commerce could all be merged into a new Department of Economic Growth, with the mission of promoting progrowth economic policies. The Department of Energy could be split into the Departments of Interior and Defense. And the Department of Education could be block granted back to the states, since education is primarily a state and local function.

All forms of corporate welfare should be thoroughly eradicated from the budget. That would include all agriculture subsidies left

Based on the historical record, we should be completing our second year of a booming recovery by now.

over from the New Deal era 75 years ago. There is no reason why farming and agriculture cannot operate without taxpayer subsidies just like any other business. Most crops, in fact, do. That would also include all of President Obama's "green" energy subsidies for wind, solar, and other alternative fuels, now amounting to tens of billion per year – and slated to explode further – and all other subsidies for any form of energy. Let them all compete, and let the consumers in the marketplace decide what and who survives. It would also include stale programs such as the Overseas Private Investment Corporation (OPIC) and the Export-Import Bank, which raid taxpayer funds to support job creation overseas.

Other outdated programs should be privatized, such as National Public Radio, the Corporation for Public Broadcasting, Amtrak, the U.S. Postal Service, and Fannie Mae and Freddie Mac. Excessive federal landholdings should also be sold off to raise funds to pay down the national debt. Even President Obama's own debt commission proposed reducing the federal workforce by 10 percent and freezing federal pay for several years. In fact, federal discretionary spending could be frozen entirely until the budget is balanced.

Further sharp reductions in federal spending would result from fundamental entitlement reforms, as I also explain in detail in *America's Ticking Bankruptcy Bomb.* The enormously successful 1996 reform of the old New Deal-era Aid to Families with Dependent Children (AFDC) program could be extended to all other federal means-tested programs, block granting welfare entirely back to the states. The old AFDC program was based on a matching federal-funding formula that paid each state more as the state spent more. The incentives for the state bureaucrats were transformed, with the federal funding provided instead through finite federal block grants that left states paying for higher costs but fully enjoying any innovative savings. The incentives for the poor were transformed by requiring work from the able-bodied for the benefits.

The astounding results are well documented. Two-thirds left the welfare rolls of the old program, earning roughly 25 percent more in total income by working, which reduced poverty. But taxpayers saved more than half the costs of the old program in real dollars based on prior trends.

There are dozens of further federal/state welfare programs, including Medicaid – perhaps numbering nearly 200 – that should be reformed in exactly the same way. The states could then each adopt entirely new welfare programs providing all assistance to the able-bodied only in return for required work first.

That can eliminate virtually all of welfare's perverse incentives for nonwork and family breakup and illegitimacy, assuring ultimately higher incomes for the poor through work and marriage. Instead of paying the bottom 20 percent of income earners not to work, as today, we would be paying them to work and contribute to economic growth instead, primarily through real private sector employment rather than taxpayer-financed benefits, resulting in enormous tax savings. Indeed, with all of these welfare programs together estimated to cost more than $10 trillion over the next 10 years, the savings would be in the trillions.

Real-world, 30-year-old examples from Chile; Galveston, Texas; and the Federal Thrift Savings Plan for federal employees show how we could finance all the benefits financed today through the payroll tax through personal savings, investment, and insurance accounts instead. Because long-term market-investment returns are so much higher than what can be paid through Social

Security, which involves only tax and redistribution rather than savings and investment, future retirees would actually enjoy much higher benefits through such reform. At the same time, workers would be contributing mighty rivers of savings and investment to the economy, which would promote booming economic growth. But the long-run result would be the greatest reduction in government spending in world history, as the benefits would ultimately be moved entirely from the public sector to market financing.

What is so striking about Obamanomics is how it so doggedly pursues the opposite of every one of the planks of Reaganomics.

Deregulation. The most important and

urgent deregulatory policy for creating another economic boom is to unleash the private sector to enable it to produce a plentiful supply of low-cost energy. That would provide a lower-cost foundation for the entire economy, effectively equivalent to another major tax cut. America enjoys the resources to be the world's No. 1 oil producer, the world's No. 1 natural gas producer, the world's No. 1 coal producer, and the world's No. 1 producer of nuclear energy. The problem is that our own government has stood perversely in the way, preventing America from using its own resources to produce a reliable supply of low-cost energy. That must stop now.

The second priority is to remove authority from the EPA to impose any regulation of so-called greenhouse gases to counter so-called global warming. As the discussion above showed, the science does not support the allegation that human activity is causing potentially catastrophic global warming, and such regulation would just impose massive, unnecessary costs on the economy. The entire EPA statutory mandate should then be amended to require it to conduct a thorough cost-benefit analysis of any new environmental regulation, considering the full economic costs as well as any other costs.

Of course, the perverse Dodd-Frank financial regulatory reform legislation should be repealed as well, as should ObamaCare and all of its overwhelming health care regulations. Also slated for repeal should be Sarbanes-Oxley, which is enormously costly for the economy, to no real benefit. The regulatory excesses that contributed to the financial crisis should be repealed as well, including the Community Reinvestment Act and any authority to require mark-to-market accounting.

Finally, Congress should pass the Regulations from the Executive In Need of Scrutiny (REINS) Act, which would require major federal regulations costing more than $100 million to be approved by Congress before becoming effective.

Monetary Policy. We would maintain a stable dollar without inflation, promoting sustained economic growth, if the Fed were tethered to a price rule in its conduct of monetary policy. That means the Fed would be guided by market prices for gold, silver, oil, and other key commodities, as well as the dollar, in determining monetary policy. When these prices started to rise, the Fed would cut back on money creation. When they fell, the Fed would accelerate money supply growth.

This would effectively equate the supply of money in dollars with the money demand for dollars. That policy maximizes investment, promoting economic growth and jobs, because investors know the value of their

---

The multiple taxation of capital discourages investment, which is what creates jobs and bids up wages by making workers more productive.

---

investments will be maintained without depreciation due to inflation or a declining value of the dollar. It also minimizes cyclical recessions that might crash their investments, as we saw with little or no recessionary cycles during the 25-year boom from 1982 to 2007. We should also explore further anchoring the dollar to gold.

This is a complete agenda to restore the American Dream of world-leading economic prosperity. With Reaganomics as a model, we can reverse course from the gathering Obama depression to another generation-long economic boom.

First American edition published in 2011 by Encounter Books, an activity of Encounter for Culture and Education, Inc., a nonprofit, tax exempt corporation.
Encounter Books website address: www.encounterbooks.com

Manufactured in the United States and printed on acid-free paper. The paper used in this publication meets the minimum requirements of ANSI/NISO Z39.48–1992 (R 1997) (*Permanence of Paper*).

FIRST AMERICAN EDITION

LIBRARY OF CONGRESS CATALOGING-IN-PUBLICATION DATA

Ferrara, Peter, 1955–
Obama and the crash of 2013 / by Peter Ferrara.
p. cm.— (Encounter broadsides)
Includes bibliographical references and index.
ISB-13: 978-1-59403-624-8 (pbk. : alk. paper)
ISBN-10: 1-59403-624-1 (pbk. : alk. paper)
1. Taxation—United States—History—21st century. 2. Fiscal policy—United States—History—21st century. 3. United States—Economic policy—2009– I. Title.
HJ2381.F4547 2011
330.973—dc23
2011039459

10 9 8 7 6 5 4 3 2 1